LITTLE NUMBERS

AND PICTURES THAT SHOW JUST HOW LITTLE THEY ARE!

By Edward Packard

Illustrated by Salvatore Murdocca

The Millbrook Press
Brookfield, Connecticut

For Sam, David, and Amy
E.P.

To my generous friend, Paul Brizzi
S.M.

Library of Congress Cataloging-in-Publication Data
Packard, Edward, 1931 –
Little numbers : and pictures that show just how little they are / by Edward Packard ; illustrated by
Salvatore Murdocca.
p. cm.
ISBN 0-7613-1904-2 (lib. bdg.) — ISBN 0-7613-1397-4 (trade)
1. Fractions—Juvenile literature. [1. Fractions.] I. Murdocca, Sal, ill. II. Title.
QA117 .P145 2001
513.2'6—dc21   00-065508

Published by The Millbrook Press, Inc.
2 Old New Milford Road
Brookfield, Connecticut   06804

Did you know there are
numbers even smaller than

three
two
and one?

How little are they?
How little can they get?

This book shows you.

We'll start **big** — with the number **1**.

You might think that there aren't any numbers smaller than one, but in this book you'll see numbers that are smaller than one, smaller than a half (1/2), smaller than a quarter (1/4), and even smaller than an eighth (1/8). **Much** smaller!

The seismosaurus may have been the longest dinosaur that ever lived. This one is 132 feet (about 40 meters) long.

A penny is worth a tenth as much as a dime, but only a hundredth as much as a dollar.

A hundredth of a meter is called a centimeter.

CRICKET

A seismosaurus shrunk to a ten-thousandth of its size is no bigger than a tiny ant.

WHO'S HOLDING THE MAGNIFIER?

I THINK IT'S MAGICAL.

RUFF! WHERE DID THAT GIANT CRICKET COME FROM?

A snail can run a ten-thousandth as fast as a cheetah.

BUT YOU ONLY HAVE ONE FOOT!

LET'S RACE.

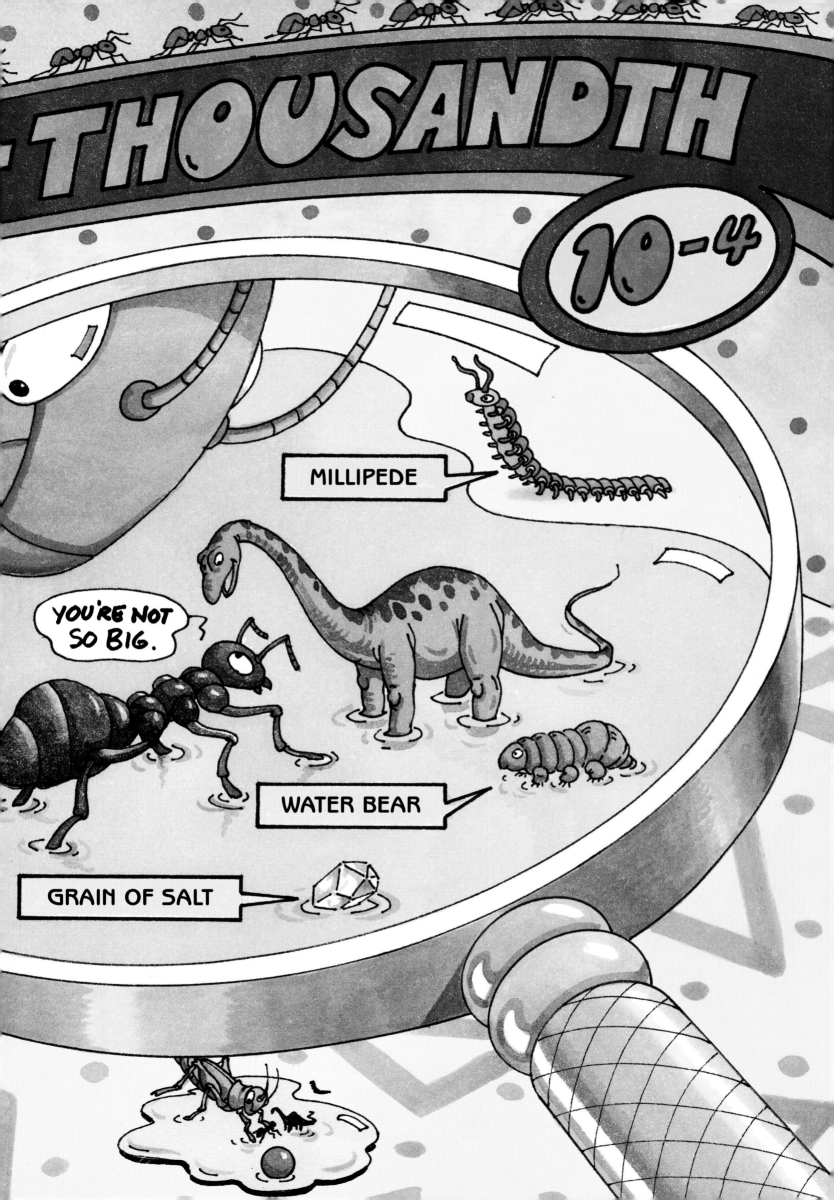

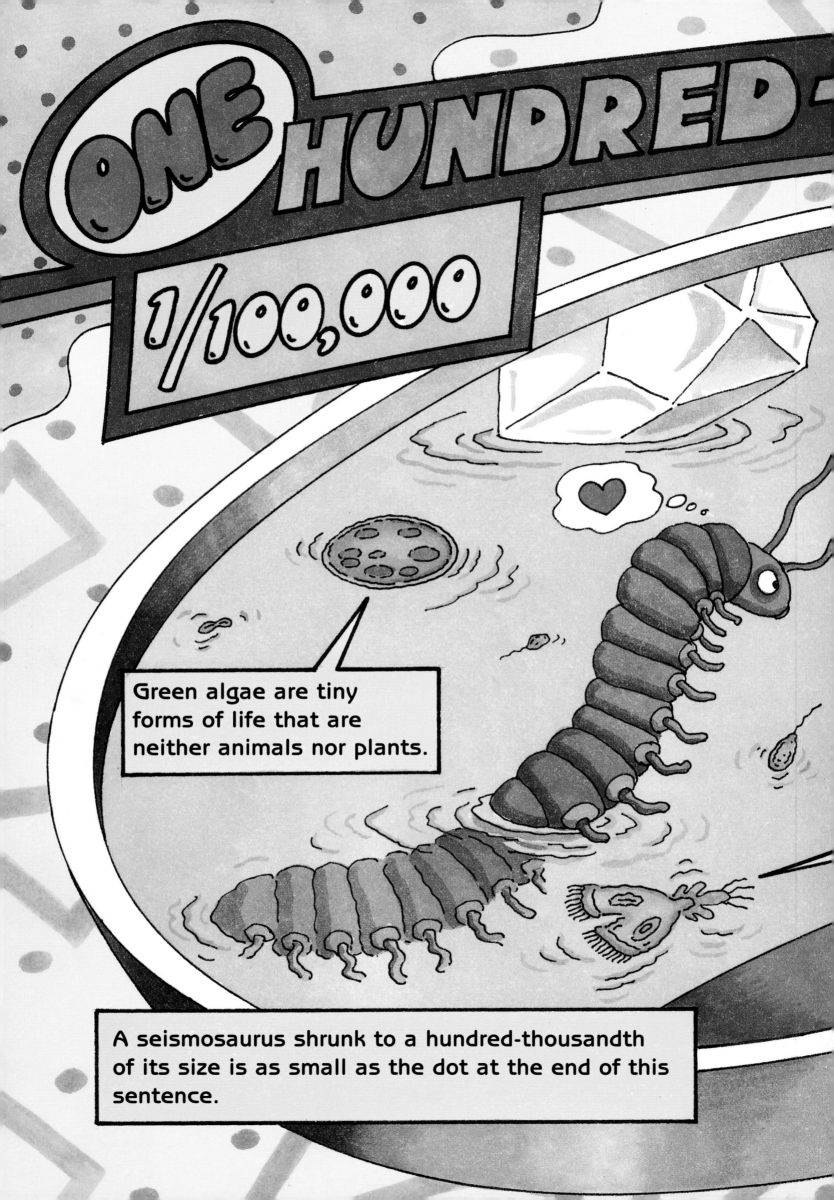

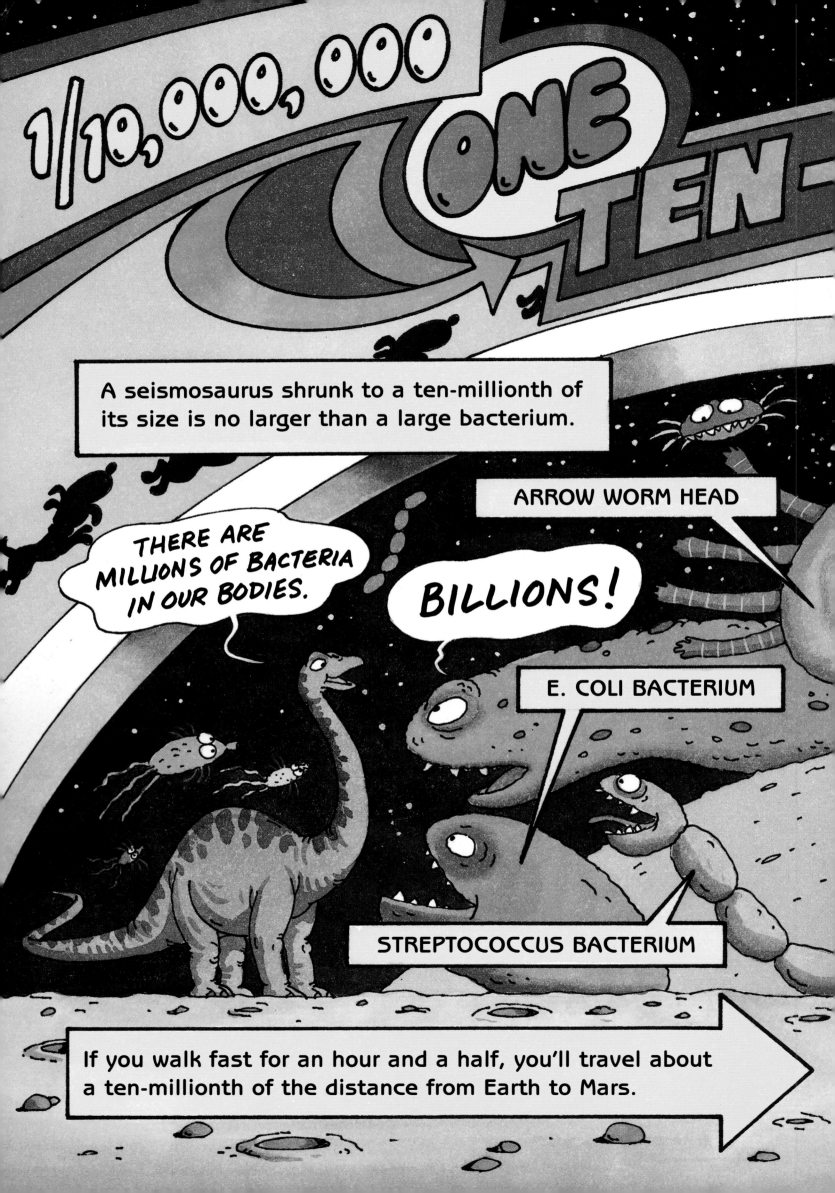

MILLIONTH
10^{-7}
Bacteria cells are simpler, and usually smaller, than cells of animals and plants.
BREAD MOLD
POLLEN GRAIN
HOW FAR DID WE COME?
ABOUT FIFTY MILLION MILES.

$1/1,000,000,000$

10^{-9}

A molecule is the smallest amount of a thing. It is made up of one or more atoms. An atom is a basic building block of everything.

If you take a single step, you'll travel about a billionth of the distance from Earth to the moon.

UH-OH!

The distance from the front end to the back end of a ladybug is about six billionths of the distance around the world.

A seismosaurus shrunk to a ten-billionth of its size is even smaller than a hemoglobin molecule.

HEMOGLOBIN MOLECULE

SALT CRYSTAL

The salt crystal is made of only two types of atoms—sodium and chlorine. That's why another name for salt is sodium chloride.

A seismosaurus shrunk to a hundred-billionth of its size is not much bigger than a water molecule.

HA! I'M YEARS AWAY!

WHERE ARE WE GOING?

TO ALPHA CENTAURI. IT'S ONLY 26 TRILLION MILES AWAY!

I'M CLOSER.

In thirty minutes, a jet plane can fly a hundred-billionth of the distance from Earth to the nearest star.

BILLIONTH

1/100,000,000,000

10^{-11}

YOU MAKE ME THIRSTY.

WATER MOLECULE

GOLD ATOM

Atoms often join together to make a molecule. For example, a water molecule is made of two atoms of hydrogen and one atom of oxygen.

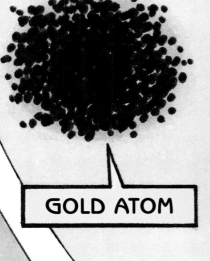

ONE TRILLIONTH

A seismosaurus shrunk to a trillionth of its size is smaller than the smallest atom.

ELECTRON

PROTON

HYDROGEN ATOM

What is the smallest number there is?

There isn't any. The numbers just keep getting smaller, and smaller, and smaller. . .

For example, the distance from the front end to the back end of a ladybug is about a million-billion-trillionths of the distance to the nearest galaxy. That's

1/1,000,000,000,000,000,000,000,000,000

or

10^{-27}

And that's just the beginning of how little little numbers can get. You could count forever and never count them all.